# Little Hymns™

**Little Hymns • *Jesus Loves Me***
Written and illustrated by Andy Holmes
Watercolor by Cameron Thorp and Matt Taylor
Music transcription by Marty Franks

Copyright ©1992 by HSH Educational Media Company
P.O. Box 167187, Irving, Texas 75016

First Printing 1992
ISBN 0-929216-55-5
Printed in the United States of America

**Published by**

**PRESS**

# Little Hymns™

by Andy Holmes

## Jesus Loves Me

Je - sus loves me! this I know,

For    the    Bi - ble    tells    me    so;

Lit - tle    ones    to    Him    be  -  long;

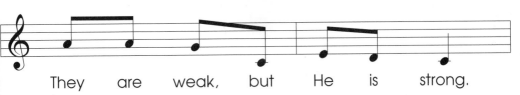

They are weak, but He is strong.

Yes, Je-sus loves me, Yes, Je-sus loves me,

Yes, Je-sus loves me, The Bi-ble tells me so.

Je - sus loves me! He who died,

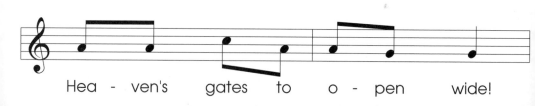

Hea - ven's gates to o - pen wide!

He will wash a - way my sin,

Let His Lit - tle child come in.

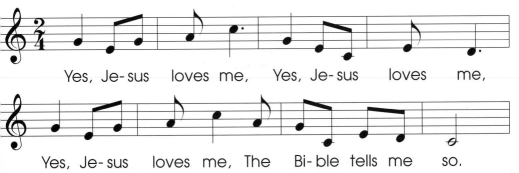

Yes, Je-sus loves me, Yes, Je-sus loves me,

Yes, Je-sus loves me, The Bi-ble tells me so.

Je - sus loves the chil - dren dear,

Chil - dren far a - way or near.

They are safe when in His care,

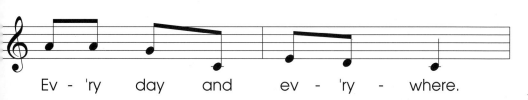

Ev - 'ry day and ev - 'ry - where.

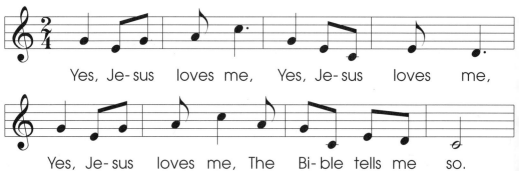

Yes, Je-sus loves me, Yes, Je-sus loves me,

Yes, Je-sus loves me, The Bi-ble tells me so.

Je - sus, take this heart of mine,

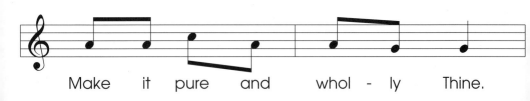

Make it pure and whol - ly Thine.

Thou   hast   bled   and   died   for   me.

I will hence - forth live for Thee.

Yes, Je-sus loves me, Yes, Je-sus loves me,

Yes, Je-sus loves me, The Bi-ble tells me so.

# Jesus Loves Me